EAGLES
LONG ROAD OUT OF EDEN

Management: Irving Azoff
Special Thanks to: Richard Davis, Steuart Smith and Lisa Thomas
Art Direction and Design: Jeri Heiden
Logo: Nick Steinhardt / SMOG Design, Inc.
Photography: Olaf Heine

www.eaglesband.com

Alfred Publishing Co., Inc.
16320 Roscoe Blvd., Suite 100
P.O. Box 10003
Van Nuys, CA 91410-0003
alfred.com

ISBN-10: 1-7390-5020-6
ISBN-13: 978-1-7390-5020-0

CONTENTS

NO MORE WALKS IN THE WOOD

Words and Music by
DON HENLEY, STEUART SMITH
and JOHN HOLLANDER

*Recording sounds two and a half steps higher than written.
Acous. Gtr. w/capo V (All frames relative to capo).

HOW LONG

Words and Music by
J.D. SOUTHER

Moderately fast ♩ = 138

Verse 1:

29106

10

nev - er__ see__ the good old__ days__ shin - ing__ in the sun__

I'll be do-ing fine,____ and then_ some.

Chorus:

How____ long, how____ long – wom - an will you weep?_

hold - - - - - - - - |

How____ long, how____ long?

hold - - - |

Verse 2:

32 *Elec. Gtr. 2 & Acous. Gtr. resume verse fig. simile*

14

How___ long, how___ long? Rock your-self to sleep___

Guitar Solo:

Verse 3:

16

*Elec. Gtr.1 dbld. by 12-string elec. gtr.

BUSY BEING FABULOUS

Words and Music by
DON HENLEY, GLENN FREY
and STEUART SMITH

Easy country rock ♩ = 104

Intro:

Verse 1:

24

just too bus-y be-ing fab - u - lous,___ uh - huh.___

the life of the par-ty But now, my ba-by — the joke is on you. And you were

Busy Being Fabulous - 12 - 10
29106

Chorus:

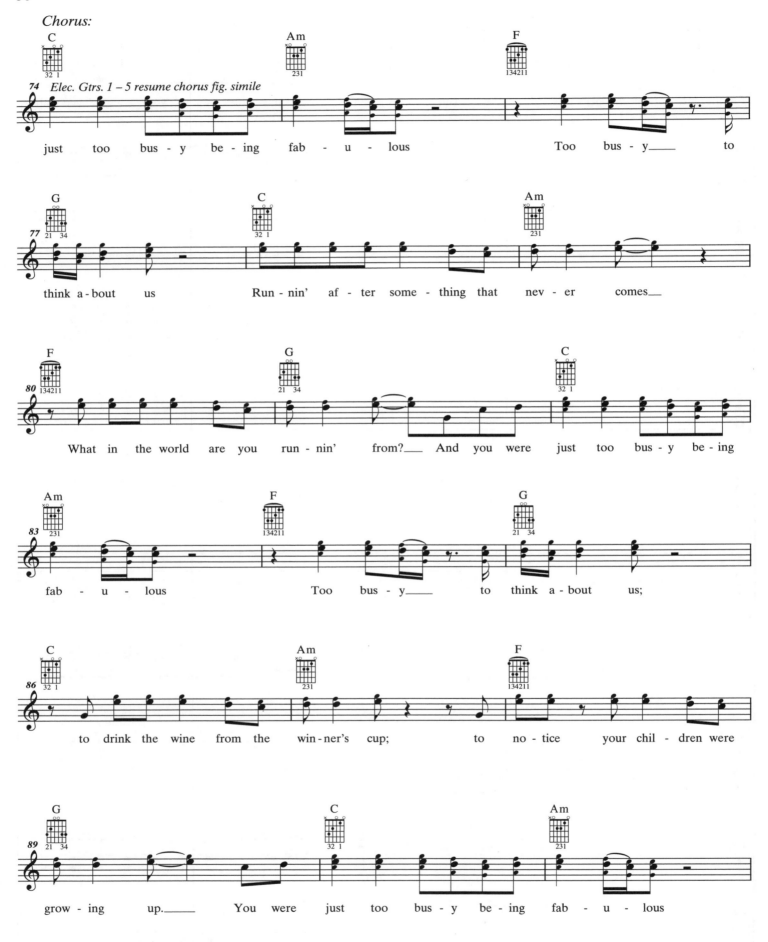

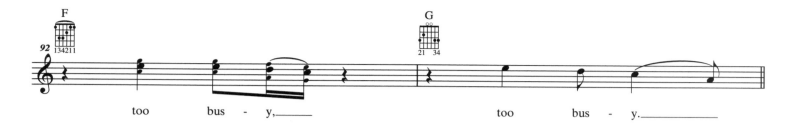

too bus - y,_____ too bus - y._____

Outro:

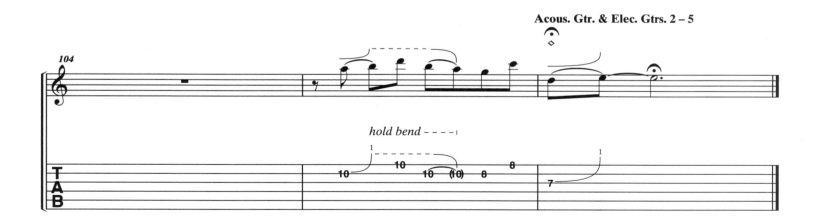

WHAT DO I DO WITH MY HEART

Words and Music by
GLENN FREY and DON HENLEY

GUILTY OF THE CRIME

Words and Music by
FRANKIE MILLER and JERRY LYNN WILLIAMS

38

Verse 2:

w/Rhy. Fig. 1 *(Elec. Gtr. 2) simile*

to - tal strang - er knock - ing at___ your___ door___ No need to

wor - ry 'bout___ the way_____ I was_ be - fore___ It's a

new love sto - ry so read ev - ery line___ You be the

judge and the ju - ry – I'm guilt - y of___ the crime.___ I'm

Guitar Solo:

Interlude:
All gtrs. tacet

I'm

Verse 3:
Elec. Gtr. 1 w/ad lib. slide guitar fills
(use previous verses and guitar solo as a model for improv.)

Elec. Gtr. 2 & Acous. Gtr. resume verse fig. simile

sav - ing all_____ my lov - ing just__ for you_____ 'Cause there's noth -

- ing more__ that I_____ would rath - er do.__ It's a

new love sto - ry got to read ev - ery line__ You be the

judge and the ju - ry – I'm guilt - y of__ the crime.__ I'm

Chorus:
Elec. Gtr. 1 cont. ad lib. slide guitar fills

Elec. Gtr. 2 & Acous. Gtr. resume chourus fig. simile

guilt - y of,__ guilt - y of__ the crime_____ of lov - ing you, ba - by

I DON'T WANT TO HEAR ANY MORE

Words and Music by
PAUL CARRACK

Verse 1:

All Elec. Gtrs. tacet

It's not__ the first__ time that I had the sense_____ that some - thing's wrong__

But I'm old e - nough_____ to know__ that things don't al - ways__ work__ out like__ they__ should__

I Don't Want to Hear Any More - 8 - 2
29106

Verse 2:

Guitar Solo:

WAITING IN THE WEEDS

Moderately ♩ = 96

Words and Music by
DON HENLEY and STEUART SMITH

*Recording sounds a half step higher than written.

**All Gtrs. w/capo I. TAB numbers and chord frames relative to capo.

Verse 1:

It's com-in' on___ the end of Au-gust An-oth-er sum-mer's prom-ise al-most___ gone___ And though I heard some wise___ man say___ that ev-'ry dog will have___ his day___ He nev-er men-tioned that___ these dog days___ get so___ long.___ 2. I don't know

Waiting in the Weeds - 11- 1
29106

54

I just watched__ it slow - ly fade__ a - way._____ 1. And
cuse me if I skip__ the mas - quer - ade._____ 2. And

Chorus:

I've been wait - ing in the weeds, – wait - ing for my
I've been wait - ing in the weeds, – wait - ing for the

Acous. Gtr. 2

Elec. Gtr.

Bridge:

I've been stum-bling through some dark plac-es, but I'm fol-low-ing the___ plow I know I've fall-en out of your good grac-es,

60

Chorus:

I've been waiting in the weeds – waiting for the summer rain to fall upon the

wild birds scattering the seeds; answering the calling of the tide's eternal

NO MORE CLOUDY DAYS

Words and Music by
GLENN FREY

Moderately ♩ = 116

Intro:

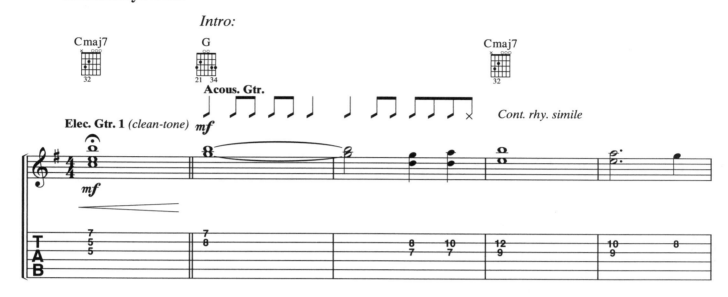

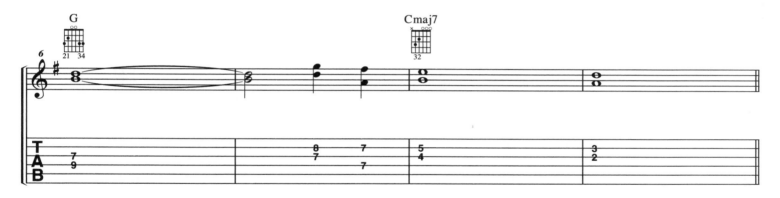

Verse 1:

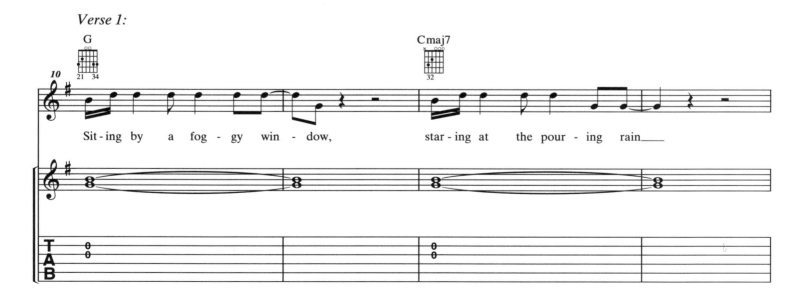

Sit-ing by a fog-gy win-dow, star-ing at the pour-ing rain___

Chorus:

no more storm - y nights___ — no more cloud - y days.___

Outro:
w/ad lib. saxophone

Rhy. Fig. 1

end Rhy. Fig. 1

w/Rhy. Fig. 1 *(Elec. Gtr. 1)*

Elec. Gtr. 2 *(clean-tone w/delay)*

P.M.

Repeat and fade

(P.M.)

No More Cloudy Days - 6 - 6
29106

FAST COMPANY

Moderately ♩ = 100

Words and Music by
DON HENLEY and GLENN FREY

*Two gtrs. arr. for one.

72

Chorus:

E5

Fast___ com-pa-ny, fast___ com-pa-ny You're go-in' no-where,

Elec. Gtr. 2

Elec. Gtr. 1

you're go-in' no-where___ fast___ Fast___ com-pa-ny, fast___ com-pa-ny

Elec. Gtr. 6 *(clean-tone)*

mp

hold throughout

Fast Company - 9 - 4
29106

You're go - in' no - where, you're go - in' no - where____ fast____

Bridge:

DO SOMETHING

Words and Music by
DON HENLEY, TIMOTHY B. SCHMIT
and STEUART SMITH

YOU ARE NOT ALONE

Words and Music by
GLENN FREY

LONG ROAD OUT OF EDEN

Words and Music by
DON HENLEY, GLENN FREY and
TIMOTHY B. SCHMIT

Long Road Out of Eden - 20 - 1
29106

Verse 2:

94

Cap - tains of the Old Or - der cling - ing to the reins   As - sur - ing us___ these aches in - side are

on - ly grow - ing pains   But it's a long   road_____ out of E -

Bridge:

home I was so___ cer-tain The path was___ ver-y clear. But now I have to won-der: What

are we do-ing here?___ I'm not count-ing on to-mor-row and I can't tell wrong from right But

*Bend string and, while holding bend, tap fret 12 with right-hand index finger and
pull off with right-hand index finger, then release bend and pull off to fret 5.

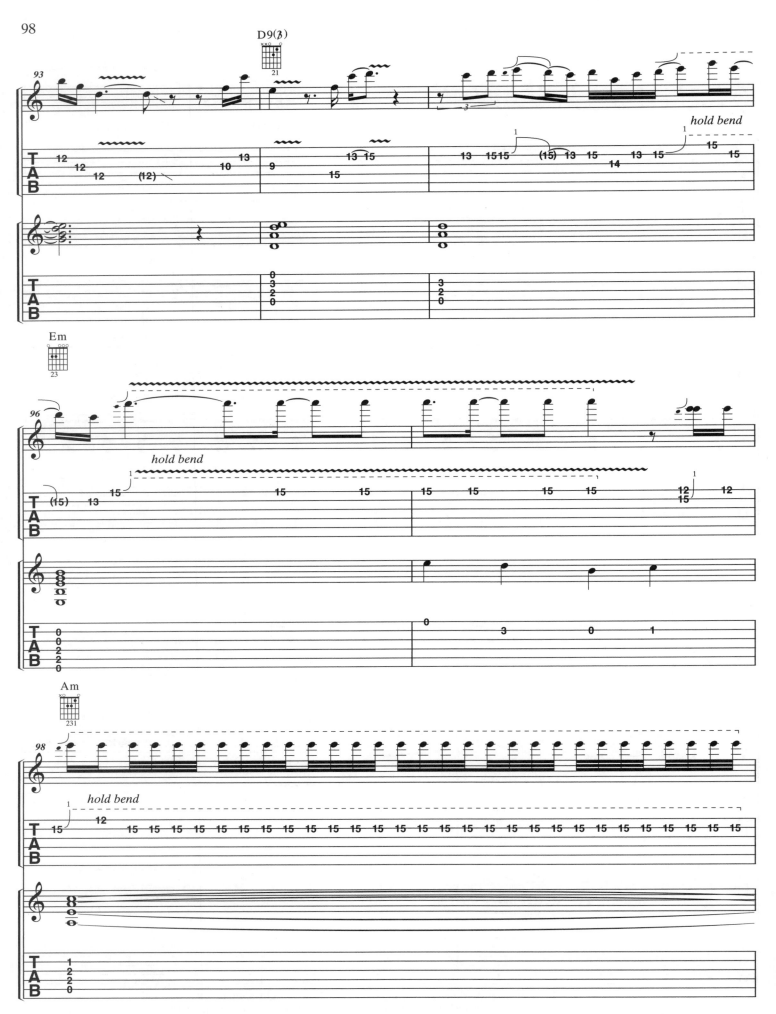

*Harmonizer effect added.

Band tacet

Wind effect and woodwind
instruments (6:15–6:40)

*Artificial Harmonic. Fret and hold strings 3, 2 & 1 at fret 5 and, using first finger of right hand,
lightly glide across fret 17 while picking strings 3, 2 & 1 with right-hand thumb.

Verse 3:

Weav-ing down the A-mer-i-can high-way Through the lit-ter and the wreck-age and the cul-tur-al junk Bloat-ed with en-ti-tle-ment; load-ed___ pro-pa-gan-da

Chorus 3:

Interlude:
Band tacet 8 meas.

Outro:

Long Road Out of Eden - 20 - 20
29106

I DREAMED THERE WAS NO WAR

Music by
GLENN FREY

*Chords implied by synth.

SOMEBODY

Words and Music by
JACK TEMPCHIN and JOHN BRANNEN

*Baritone Gtr. tuning: ⑥ = A; ⑤ = D; ④ = A; ③ = D; ② = G; ① = B
Sounds 1 octave lower than written.

**Elec. Gtr. 1 w/Drop D: ⑥ = D.

Somebody - 8 - 1
29106

Verse 1:
Elec. Gtrs. tacet

but not___ bad e - nough___ You know you got it

com-ing 'cause you played so rough Back o - ver your shoul -

Somebody - 8 - 2
29106

114

Chorus 2 & 3:
w/Rhy. Figs. 2 (Elec. Gtr. 2) & 2A (Elec. Gtr. 1) both 2 times

*Elec. Gtr. 4 (clean-tone)

*Elec. Gtr. 4 standard tuning.

Somebody - 8 - 5
29106

*Elec. Gtr. 5 in Open E tuning: ⑥ = E; ⑤ = B; ④ = E; ③ = G#; ② = B; ① = E

116

D.S. % al Coda

3. There's a   jack - o' - lan - tern

Coda

w/Rhy. Figs. 1 *(Baritone Gtr.)* **& 1A** *(Elec. Gtr. 1)*

Some - bod - y,

Elec. Gtr. 5

w/slide

Baritone Gtr.

you know there's some - bod - y,

ooh.

FRAIL GRASP ON THE BIG PICTURE

Words and Music by
DON HENLEY, GLENN FREY
and STEUART SMITH

w/Rhy. Figs. 1 *(Elec. Gtr. 1)* **& 1 A** *(Elec. Gtr. 2)*

Elec. Gtr. 4 *(w/talk box effect)*

Verse 1:

w/Rhy. Fig. 1A *(Elec. Gtr. 2) 4 times*

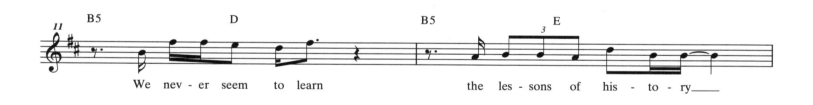

Well, ain't it a shame_____ 'bout our short___ lit - tle mem - o - ry

We nev - er seem to learn the les - sons of his - to - ry_____

We keep mak - ing the same___ mis - takes___ — o - ver and o - ver and o - ver and o - ver a -

gain And then we won - der why___ we're in the shape we're in.___

Chorus:

end Rhy. Fig. 2

Frail__ grasp__ on the Big__ Pic-ture Light__ fad-ing and the

fog is get-ting thick-er Frail__ grasp__ on the Big__ Pic-ture

Elec. Gtr. 6 (w/light dist.)

Elec. Gtr. 7 (w/light dist.)

Elec. Gtrs. 4 & 7

That ain't what's go-ing on

Jour-nal-ism__ dead and gone.__

122

'n' soul-ful con-ver-sa-tion that go on un-til the dawn___

How man-y times___ can you tell your sto-ry? How man-y hang-o-vers

can you en-dure___ – just to get some snog-ging done?

You're liv-ing in a hor-mone dream___ You don't have the slight-est no-tion

Guitar Solo:

Outro:

Frail___ grasp___ on the

Big___ Pic - ture.

Frail___ grasp___ on the Big___ Pic - ture.

Elec. Gtr. 3

Elec. Gtr. 4

Frail Grasp on the Big Picture - 14 - 14
29106

LAST GOOD TIME IN TOWN

Words and Music by
JOE WALSH and J.D. SOUTHER

*Chords are implied by electric piano.

(2nd time only)

Guitar Solo:

*w/harmonizer effect.

Coda

last good time in town.___

Elec. Gtr. 1

Outro:

I LOVE TO WATCH A WOMAN DANCE

Waltz ♩ = 130

Words and Music by
LARRY JOHN McNALLY

Verse 1:

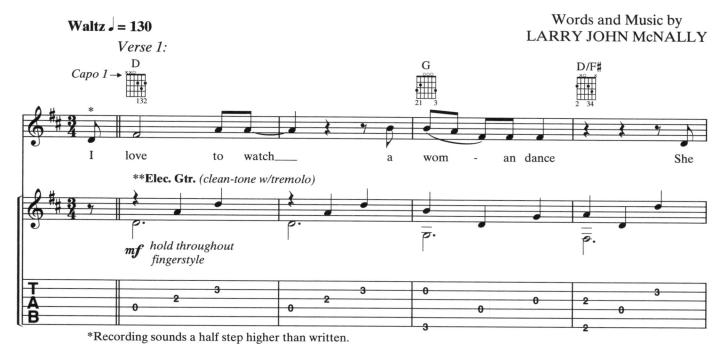

Recording sounds a half step higher than written.

**Elec. Gtr. w/capo I. Chord frames and TAB numbers relative to capo.*

I love to watch a wom - an dance She bows Her head and lifts her hands Her hips be - gin to cir - cle slow - ly Her

eyes half closed – her face is ho - ly She holds the whole room in a trance I love to watch a wom - an dance Yeah, I love to watch a wom - an

I Love to Watch a Woman Dance - 8 - 2
29106

I Love to Watch a Woman Dance - 8 - 3
29106

long as I can_____ 'Cause, who knows, this dance may be____ our on - ly

dance.____

So we

Verse 3:

Mandolin tacet

Elec. Gtr. resume verse fig. simile

dance_____ to - geth - er close and slow –

I Love to Watch a Woman Dance - 8 - 6
29106

BUSINESS AS USUAL

Words and Music by
DON HENLEY and STEUART SMITH

Moderately fast ♩ = 126

Intro:

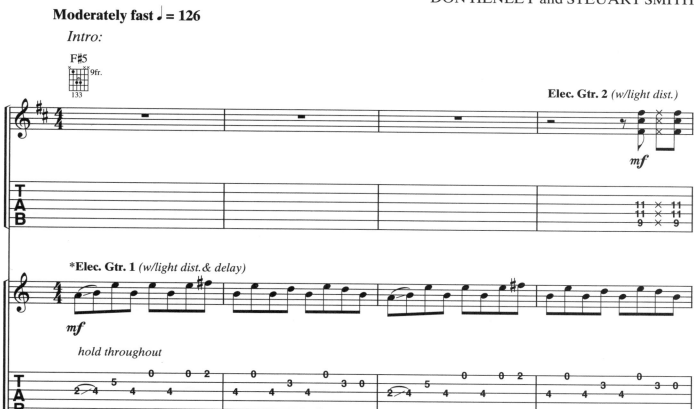

*Elec. Gtr. 1 w/capo II. TAB numbers relative to capo.
Elec. Gtr. 1 sounds one whole step higher than written.

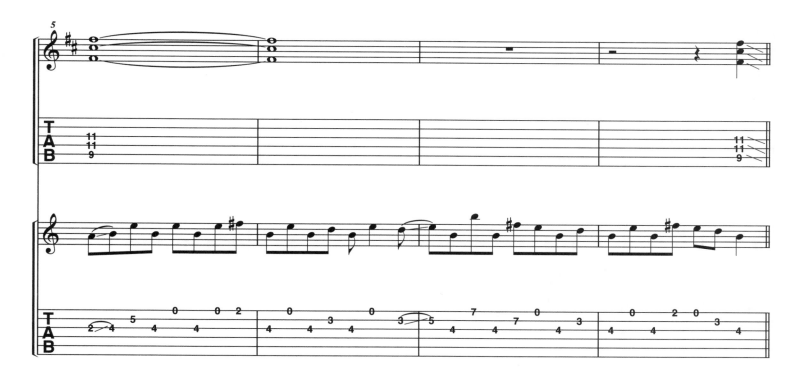

Business As Usual - 15 - 1
29106

148

Verse:

1. Look at the weath - er
2. Mon - u - ments to ar - ro - gance;

Look at the news
reach for the sky.

Rhy. Fig. 1A
Elec. Gtr. 2

Rhy. Fig. 1B
Elec. Gtr. 3 (w/light dist.)

slight P.M. throughout

Look at all the peo - ple in de - ni -
Our bet - ter na - tures bur - ied in the rub -

Elec. Gtr. 4 (w/light dist. & delay)

mf (2nd time only)

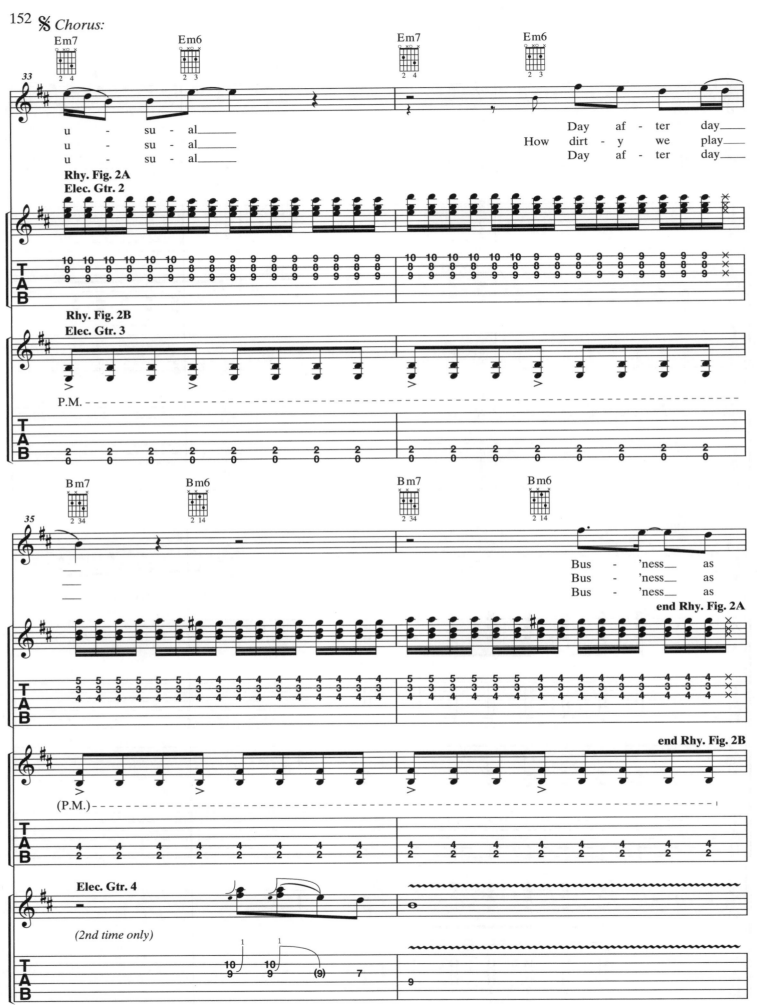

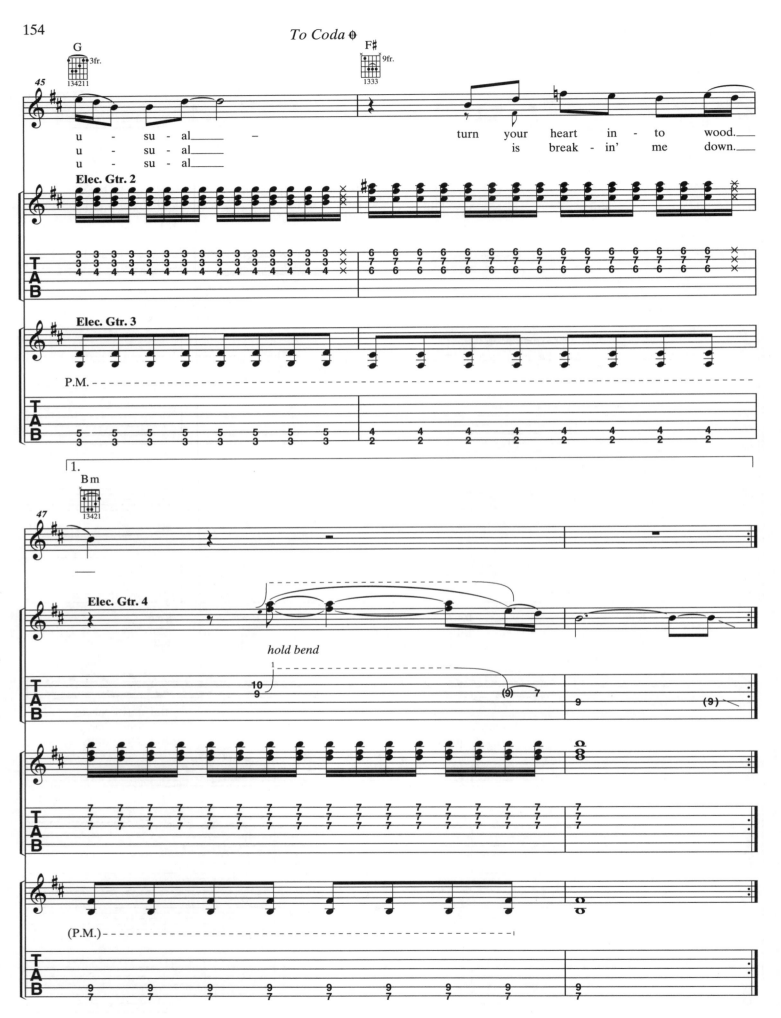

Guitar Solo:

Outro:
w/Rhy. Figs. 1A *(Elec. Gtr. 2)* **& 1B** *(Elec. Gtr. 3)*

Elec. Gtrs. 2 & 3

CENTER OF THE UNIVERSE

Words and Music by
DON HENLEY, STEUART SMITH
and GLENN FREY

Slowly ♩ = 60

Intro:

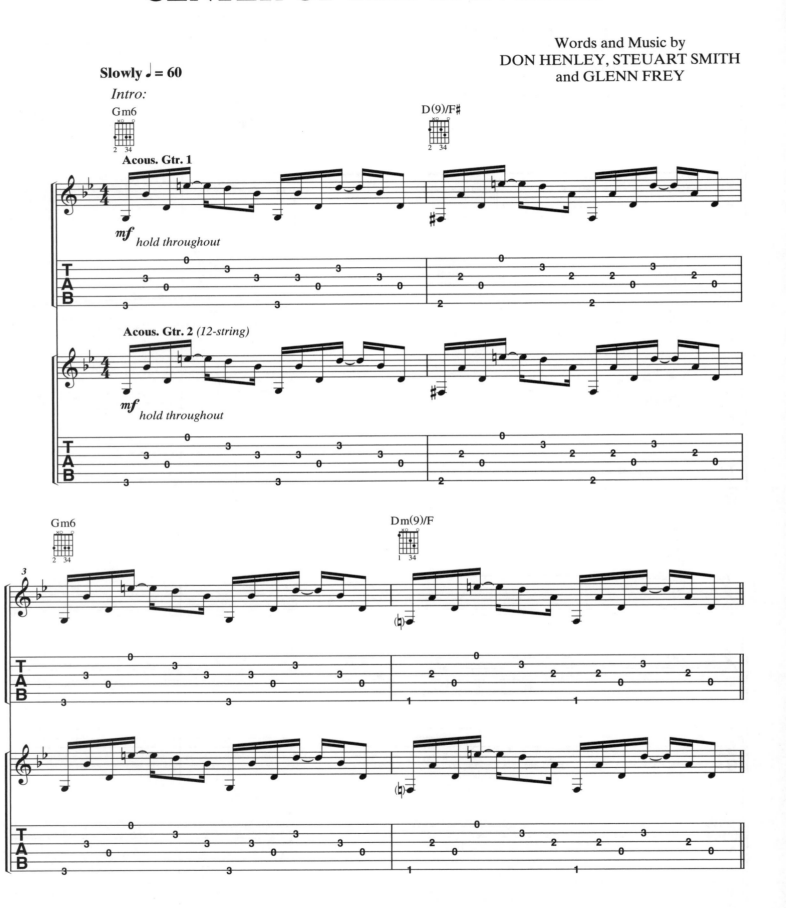

Center of the Universe - 5 - 1
29106

Verse 1:

IT'S YOUR WORLD NOW

Words and Music by
GLENN FREY and JACK TEMPCHIN

It's Your World Now - 6 - 1
29106

It's Your World Now - 6 - 3
29106